Echoes Of The Mind

A Psychiatrist's Poetic Journal

Dr Amisha Vashisht

BookLeaf Publishing

India | USA | UK

Made with ❤ on the BookLeaf Publishing Platform
www.bookleafpub.in
www.bookleafpub.com

Dedication

"To my mentors, my patients, and the unseen struggles of the mind—this book is for you."

Preface

Psychiatry is not just a field of medicine—it is a realm of stories, where reality bends, perceptions deceive, and the mind itself becomes both the mystery and the key.

As a resident doctor in psychiatry, I have witnessed moments of sheer brilliance, profound despair, and the surreal beauty of the human psyche unraveling and healing.

This book is a collection of those moments—the diagnoses that left me in awe, the patients who challenged my understanding, and the strange, poetic nature of mental illness itself. Each poem is a glimpse into the world of psychiatry, not just as a science, but as an experience.

Mental illness is often misunderstood, feared, or dismissed—but in these pages, **it demands to be seen.**
Welcome to the mind's poetry.
Welcome to psychiatry.

Acknowledgements

This book is a reflection of the minds I have met, the stories I have witnessed, and the marvel that psychiatry evokes every day.

To my mentors,

For proving that sharp wit and sharper diagnoses can coexist, possessing an uncanny ability to diagnose from the subtlest clues, unraveling complexities others might overlook.

For being a force of intelligence and strength, for showing me the balance between resilience and compassion, and for leading by example in a field that demands both.

To my patients,

The ones who walked into the hospital with fear, doubt, and pain, and in turn, left me with stories that shaped my understanding of the human mind. Thank you for your trust, for your resilience, and for teaching me more than any textbook ever could.

To my colleagues,

For endless discussions, and the shared fascination for the surreal world of psychiatry. The journey is easier when walked alongside people who truly understand it.

To my family and friends,

For their support, patience, and belief in my work. To my father who truly inspired me to compose & compile my verses. Special acknowledgement is reserved for my son Kevin. His love, boundless energy, and infectious enthusiasm have been the driving force behind my motivation & accomplishments. It is with a profound sense of pride and fulfillment that I dedicate this book to him.

To psychiatry itself,

For being a world where science meets poetry, and where every patient is a story waiting to be understood. And to **you**, the reader—may these words make you see, feel, and wonder.

With gratitude,
Dr. Amisha Vashisht
DNB Psychiatry Resident

1. The Woman Who Wanted to Die—And Then Wanted to Fly

She sat in the ward, wrapped in despair,
A hollow gaze, a vacant stare.
Bruises bloomed where her hands had hit,
A silent war, no cease, no quit.

"I don't want to live," she whispered low,
"I don't deserve, I cannot go."
Her head met the wall, a dull, rhythmic sound,
A grief so heavy, it pulled her down.

She spoke of children only she could see,
A boy and a girl, haunting, unfree.
"You're filthy," they sneered, *"it was your fault,"*
Ghosts of the past, chained in assault.

Her father—a shadow, a nightmare in flesh,
Her mother—a silence, a wound still fresh.

No arms had held, no voice had soothed,
A life of echoes, jagged and bruised.

Each morning, I sat by her bed,
Fighting the darkness locked in her head.
Words felt useless, medicine slow,
What do you say to a soul sunk low?

And then—one day—the ground trembled beneath,
Not with sorrow, but something unleashed.
It wasn't a slow ascent, a gentle reprieve,
But an eruption—a force, wild and free.

She walked, no—she *floated* across the floor,
Lipstick red, lined eyes sharp as war.
Braids twisted in intricate thread,
A queen emerging where ghosts once tread.

"Look at me!" she laughed, spinning with glee,
"I've been wasting my time in bed, can't you see?"
Her voice was a song, electric and bright,
A wildfire consuming the remnants of night.

She spoke of plans, of places to be,
Of dancing on rooftops, of running to the sea.
"I've been chosen, don't you know?" she declared,

"I have things to do, I have dreams to be shared!"

A nurse gently placed a hand on her arm,
But she twirled away, untouched, unharmed.
"I don't need rest, I don't need sleep—"
Her body alive with a fever too deep.

She glided through halls, a queen in her reign,
Dripping in brilliance, unchained from pain.
And I? A mere scribe, lost in her flight,
Watching her slip into untamed light.

I should have felt relief—
This was a victory, wasn't it?
The girl who once whispered now burned with light,
The pendulum swung, left despair behind.

But I knew better.
Beneath the laughter, the kohl-lined gaze,
Lay the same restless, frenzied maze.

From the cliffs of sorrow, she'd leapt too high,
Trading the depths for a manic sky.

I marveled, I worried, I watched her soar,
Knowing that storms come after war.

Would she keep rising, defying the fall?
Or would the same gravity take her after all?

Bipolar—a tempest, a thief in the night,
One moment drowning, the next in flight.
But in that swing, in that fearless smile,
For a moment—just a moment—she was alive.

____

This poem captures the sheer marvel and bewilderment
of witnessing bipolar disorder in motion—the abrupt
shift from crippling despair to mania. It portrays the
intoxicating rise, and the lurking inevitability of the fall.

2. The Girl They Called Borderline

She walked in loud, her colors bright,
A rebel draped in neon light.
Electric blue streaked through her hair,
A challenge whispered in her stare.

Her nails were chipped, her hands too thin,
Old scars lay faint beneath her skin.
A bracelet clung, worn and tight,
Not strong enough to hide the fight.

She slumped into the waiting chair,
Legs still bouncing, fingers bare.
Her words poured fast, a tangled thread,
Spilling thoughts from a restless head.

"I feel too much, all at once."
"I lose control, I take the brunt."
"I lash, I burn, I fight, I fall,"
"Then hate myself for it all."

Her parents sighed, their patience worn,
Tired eyes, expressions torn.
"She shifts like wind, she flares, she breaks,"
"Then drowns in all the mess she makes."

"She tricks, she twists, she turns things wild,"
"We cannot reach this reckless child."
"We've read the books, we know her fate,"
"Borderline—it fits just great."

I leaned in close, my mind alight,
This wasn't a case, this was a fight.
Where others saw chaos, he saw form,
A hurricane caught inside a storm.

Then he spoke, the doctor sure,
A voice so sharp, so calm, so pure.
He leaned back slow, his gaze stayed keen,
A smirk unfolding, sharp, serene.

"Borderline? No, that's not the call,"
"That's just a label they throw on all."

The air grew thick, the girl sat tight,
Her fists still clenched, prepared for flight.
"You're wrong," she snapped, *"they all agree!"*

"Every doctor said that's me!"

But he just twirled his pen with ease,
"They saw the leaves, but not the trees."
"You don't have one, you've got three,"
"And all of them? They're treatable, see."

"ADHD—you miss the cues,"
"Drifting off, lost in the clues."
"OCD—you check, repeat,"
"A mind that loops but won't delete."
"Bipolar swings you high then low,"
"A fire, a flood, a wreck, a glow."

She blinked, then froze, the words sank in,
Like missing pieces fit within.
Her parents sat, too stunned to speak,
The weight had shifted, not so bleak.

"Unlike Borderline," he added light,
*"These three, we **can** set right."*

And just like that, the chains grew weak,
A door creaked open, change could speak.

She came back, week after week,
The blue in her hair now soft, unique.

Her scars grew faint, her hands still tapped,
But not from chaos—just relaxed.

"I exist in the present now, unlike before,"
"I don't feel like I'm caught in a war."
"The hurricane's quiet, the rush has slowed,"
"For once, I'm here—not lost, not cold."

Her parents watched, both calm, unsure,
"She still argues, but it's not a war."
"She's not perfect, but she's here to stay,"
"Is this our daughter, found today?"

And as I watched, I truly knew,
She hadn't changed—she just saw through.
She had never been broken, never been wrong,
She had only been misunderstood all along.

ADHD makes them impulsive, OCD traps them in doubt,
and Bipolar fuels the storms—together, they blur the
lines, making **Borderline Personality** *easy but wrong.*
Some labels can lock, but the right ones can set them
free.

3. The Woman Who Once Had Everything Right

She sat with shoulders drawn, hands clenched tight,
Her frail fingers tracing prayers in flight.
"I don't need a doctor," she weakly declared,
Yet her gaze, restless, was heavy and scared.

Her son sighed, her daughter-in-law spoke,
"She wakes in the morning but moves so slow.
She sits with her books, the pages untouched,
Yet she whispers she hasn't done enough.

She folds the same cloth, she counts the same beads,
Yet nothing feels right—no matter her needs.
She asks if she's prayed, she asks if it's true,
Then doubts it again and asks anew."

The doctor sat back, eyes keen and bright,
A mind that dissected without need for sight.
His fingers spun his pen with ease,
Measuring silence, unraveling unease.

Where others saw patterns, he saw the cracks,
Tracing the mind's maze, never looking back.

"Not just sadness," he murmured low,
"Not just despair, but a mind caught in woe.
A perfectionist heart, now bound by its doubt,
A mind once sharp, now caught in a rout."

Her lips trembled, voice barely a sound,
A whisper of loss, a sorrow profound.
"Mujhse bhakti bhi nahi hoti," she sighed,
"Even God must think I've failed, cast aside.
What if my prayers were said all wrong?
What if my chants were never that strong?
What if the floor I swept is still unclean?
What if I forget things I've already seen?"

Her breaths grew short, her hands gripped tight,
Her world was shrinking, drowned in white.
And when the weight became too much to bear,
She would call her husband, pull at his care.
"Recite the chants," she would beg in despair,
"For hours, don't stop, don't leave me there."

A fortress of rituals, yet never complete,
Her mind unyielding, looping defeat.
I watched as she sank, her frame bent with strife,

A prisoner of thought, a weary life.

And then—amid sorrow, a jest broke through,
The doctor smirked, his tone casual, askew.
"She's lucky, you know," he said with a glance,
Her daughter-in-law frowned, caught in a trance.
"Why?" she asked, cautious, unsure,
He leaned back, amused by the detour.

"Because, you idiot, you worry, you fuss, you care too
much,"
"An anxious heart has the softest touch."

For a moment, the old woman stopped,
Her tired face deep in thought.
Then slowly, like a fading breeze,
A shy, weary smile found release.

Not wide, not strong, but gentle and true,
A quiet warmth just passing through.
Like aged fabric, soft yet worn,
Still holding onto the dreams once born.

I watched in awe as OCD turned devotion into burden,
routine into chains. A sharp mind, once precise, now lost

in endless doubt—trapped, not by the world, but by its own design.

4. The Man Who Watched Himself Fade

He lived his life, routine and neat,
An advocate firm on steady feet.
A father, a husband, a man well-known,
Until his mind became a warzone.

One day, he paused, his breath ran tight,
"My body is shrinking, something's not right."
His hands would tremble, his face grew pale,
A horror spun into endless tale.

"My manhood fades, it's slipping away,"
"And with it, I will die someday."
Doctors chuckled, waved him aside,
"You're healthy, sir, it's in your mind."

But fear took root, a vengeful seed,
That only grew with urgent need.
He stopped all touch, withdrew from sight,
Fearing he'd vanish in the night.

His world grew dark, his body frail,
His mind set sail on sorrow's trail.
He lay in bed, too weak to stand,
Fingers tracing a phantom land.

"My stomach is broken, my legs are too,"
"My organs are rotting, I know it's true."
He whispered low, his eyes gone wide,
A prisoner locked in his own mind.

His wife would plead, her voice turned rough,
"Look, we have savings, we have enough!"
But he shook his head, dismissed her grace,
"We'll starve, we'll beg, we'll fall from place."

Twice he walked to the river's bend,
Thinking this was how it'd end.
Yet fear of half-life made him turn,
And back to bed he went to yearn.

His taste was lost, his scent grew weak,
His voice grew hollow each time he'd speak.
His teeth decayed, his limbs felt numb,
His heart, he swore, had ceased to drum.

"I am rotting, I can't be saved,"

"Let me go, just dig my grave."
He stopped his meals, refused his pills,
A body obeying what the mind instills.

"Why waste your money? Let me fade,"
"No medicine works, no progress made."
His wife stood firm, though frail with ache,
Her love the thread he'd yet to break.

They dragged him back, his frame too light,
A ghost still fighting against the night.
For twelve long years, his world was grey,
A corpse that simply wouldn't decay.

Koro took his manhood's form,
Cotard made death the lasting norm.
Two delusions, cruel and vast,
A mind erasing its own past.

And yet, he remained, though his soul felt gone,
Trapped in a world where he didn't belong.
A mind convinced it had ceased to be,
Yet bound to a body that refused to break free.

This poem encapsulates the patient's struggle Cotard syndrome (the delusion that his body was decaying or non-existent). It also touches on the profound depression, withdrawal, and self-starvation that followed.

5. A Love That Was Never There

She sat alone, her fingers tight,
Eyes burning with sleepless nights.
A world once filled with books and rhyme,
Now lost in whispers, blurred in time.

The songs she played, the words she read,
All spoke his name inside her head.
A voice so certain, an unshaken glow,
"He loves me, this, I know."

A name in lights, a distant star,
Yet she believed—not too far.
A message hidden, a secret cue,
Numbers, lyrics, signs she knew.

A story woven, pure, divine,
She was his, and he was mine.
No proof, no touch, no spoken vow,
But love was here, it lived somehow.

When others spoke, she turned away,
"They wouldn't get it anyway."
Her parents' words, her sister's sighs,
Meant nothing next to his replies.

A post, a picture, just for her,
Proof enough—it must occur.
Why else would fate align just so?
"He loves me, this, I know."

Then shadows crept, distrust took hold,
The world turned cruel, the nights grew cold.
Her food was drugged, her doors weren't locked,
They all conspired—her heart was mocked.

The love they built, the war she fought,
Now twisted into darkened thought.
A memory lost, a past erased,
A life they stole, a truth misplaced.

"They're watching me, they read my mind,"
"They want to break what fate designed."
"They'll keep us apart, they want me dead,"
"But he will come, just like he said."

She ran, she searched, she left behind,

A world that told her love was blind.
Through empty streets, through fear's embrace,
She sought him in a stranger's place.

And when she stood, alone once more,
Waiting at a foreign door—
The love she swore would end the fight,
Did not arrive to prove her right.

Exhausted, fragile, drowning deep,
Too tired to eat, too lost to sleep.
A love so fierce, yet built on air,
A love that was never there.

Erotomania, the unwavering belief that someone—often distant, famous, or completely unaware—returns a love that never existed. It is a marvel to witness—the sheer conviction, the intricate justifications, the desperate pursuit of a love that only lived within her mind.

6. She Danced in the Rain

I saw her first in a fleeting glance,
Spinning in circles, lost in a trance.
The rain poured down, yet she gleamed with light,
A woman ablaze, too wild for the night.

Her bangles clinked as she twirled around,
Feet bare against the trembling ground.
With flowers woven through her hair,
She swayed with a joy too fierce to bear.

"I am Meera," she boldly cried,
"Krishna calls, I must abide!"
She spoke of whispers in the air,
Of signs and visions, everywhere.

Her home became a temple grand,
With incense thick and prayers unplanned.
At dawn, she sang, at dusk, she swayed,
A goddess lost, a woman frayed.

The world, she claimed, had turned unkind,
Jealous of her enlightened mind.
Her husband scolded—she simply laughed,
"You fear my bliss, you block my path!"

She adorned her lord, her golden king,
Selling her jewels to buy him rings.
The hunger gnawed, yet she didn't care,
"Food is nothing—faith is air."

The neighbors whispered, the landlord sighed,
She danced as if the stars complied.
"You cannot chain a soul set free!"
She told them all, *"Just wait and see."*

But even storms must lose their fight,
Even fires dim their light.
And so she fell, pale and thin,
A body frail, a mind caved in.

Yet still, she murmured through her pain,
"Let me dance, just once again."

This poem reflects Mania's intoxicating rise and devastating fall—a woman caught between divinity and delusion, between euphoria and exhaustion. What begins as bliss spirals into chaos, a mind untamed, a soul set aflame.

7. The Weight of Empty Plates

She counted calories like they were sins,
Measuring meals in smaller bins.
A bite too much, a sip too bold,
A war with hunger, silent, cold.

It started small—a whispered jest,
A cruel remark, a playful test.
"Too big, too broad, a waste of space,"
She shrank herself to find her place.

The mirror whispered, sharp and sly,
"Not enough—keep going, try."
She climbed the stairs, she walked for miles,
Each skipped meal brought fleeting smiles.

She ran on emptiness, fueled by fear,
Her body weak, her mind unclear.
"You look unwell," they softly said,
Yet compliments danced inside her head.

Her ribs emerged, her skin grew pale,
The numbers dropped, she tipped the scale.
Yet joy turned into quiet dread—
No matter how, the weight still spread.

A school-day check—a cruel display,
The scale betrayed her secret way.
Four pounds gained, the room turned tight,
A mind unhinged, a heart in flight.

She wept, she begged, she paced, she screamed,
"Undo this all, erase this dream!"
She searched for ways, for tricks, for pain,
To carve herself back once again.

They took her hands, they made her stay,
They tried to pull her fears away.
But in her mind, the war still calls—
A battle fought with empty walls.

This poem sheds light on the relentless grip of Anorexia Nervosa, the way it begins with control and spirals into fear. It illustrates the obsession with weight, the euphoria of loss, and the despair of gain, all while

highlighting the silent suffering behind every empty
plate.

8. The Man Who Fled from Shadows

He once stood tall, a scholar bright,
A mind that soared, a future in sight.
From Nepal's hills to Delhi's haze,
He carved his path through sleepless days.

But shadows crept where dreams once lay,
A silent thief, it stole away.
First, the weight of doubt grew thick,
A mind once sharp now dull and sick.

"Why am I tired?" he wondered aloud,
The football field, once home, felt loud.
Each step was heavy, each move a chore,
The game he loved—he played no more.

Then sadness came, a nameless ache,
A heaviness he couldn't shake.
His mother's voice, once warm and near,
Now lost behind a wall of fear.

Sleep was brief, his nights were torn,
By restless thoughts and breath forlorn.
His father's health, his own disgrace,
A weight too great, a losing race.

Then whispers rose in empty air,
Familiar voices everywhere.
They mocked his name, they knew his crime,
Though he had none—he felt their rhyme.

He ran from class, he locked his door,
"They'll punish me—I know for sure."
His brother knocked, his friends would call,
But shame had built too high a wall.

Then silence fell, too thick to break,
He'd sit for hours, slow to wake.
Clothes half-worn, his meals untouched,
A life once full—now shrunk to dust.

And then, one night, the voices grew,
A chorus loud, a tale untrue.
"You are filth, you don't belong,"
"You have failed, and we are strong."

He curled up tight, he barely spoke,

Trapped inside a mind that broke.
Until the world, in white-clad care,
Reached for him—pulled him from despair.

Now he sits, his voice still low,
A man returning, slow, but so.
For shadows flee where light is cast,
And healing comes, though never fast.

This poem encapsulates a Depressive Episode with Psychotic Symptoms, capturing the slow descent from fatigue to paranoia, and the heavy weight of guilt and shame. It highlights the struggle of a brilliant mind losing its grip yet still holding on to the threads of recovery.

9. A Mother's Silence

She once stood strong, steady and sure,
A woman whose laughter was bright and pure.
But now she sat, withdrawn and low,
A shadow of the self she used to know.

The first time I saw her, her gaze was tired,
Her spirit dimmed, her joy expired.
A newborn nestled close in her lap,
Yet love felt distant, out of grasp.

The child would giggle, arms stretched wide,
But she just watched, empty inside.
The love was there, she swore it so,
Yet why did she feel so hollow below?

She lay in bed, too weak to rise,
Staring blankly at morning skies.
A bottle left unwashed, a dress unworn,
The weight of days too heavy, too worn.

The voices whispered in her ear,
"You are failing, can't you hear?"
"A wife unloved, a mother untrue,"
"A daughter burdening the ones who knew."

She stopped the calls, she turned away,
Avoided mirrors, night and day.
The meals grew small, the sleep was thin,
A fading ghost beneath her skin.

And when they came, with gentle hands,
She shook her head at their demands.
"You don't know," she wept, *"you can't understand."*
"I am lost in a life I once had planned."

Yet through the sorrow, the weight, the strife,
Hope flickered still—a thread of life.
A voice that said, **you are still here,**
A love that waits, a light drawn near.

____

This poem unravels Postpartum Depression, the silent suffering of a mother who feels disconnected, overwhelmed, and burdened with guilt. It highlights the slow descent into exhaustion, self-doubt, and emotional numbness, yet ends on the note that hope and healing are always within reach.

10. The Man Who Smoked the Sky

I watched him walk in, unchained, untamed,
A king without a throne, yet never ashamed.
His eyes burned bright, his steps were light,
Like gravity had lost its right.

"Doctor, listen—I have a gift,"
"A force within, a cosmic shift."
"One look, just one, and I will know,"
"The hearts of men, their truth will show."

His voice was silk, his hands alive,
Fingers tracing unseen signs.
"I touched the air, it spoke to me,"
"A thousand lifetimes—I finally see."

They told me it started with a drag,
A mellowed high, a harmless tag.

Just a vape, a bit of fun,
A world that blurred, a mind undone.

Then weed arrived, a fragrant dream,
Rolled in whispers, laced in green.
A puff, a laugh, the world stood still,
Then panic crashed—a broken thrill.

The days unraveled, the joints stacked high,
He smoked the sun, he smoked the sky.
Reality bent beneath his gaze,
A prophet lost in purple haze.

"They plot, they scheme, they set a snare,"
"But I have seen, I'm well aware."
"The showpieces talk, they shift, they glow,"
"I move them right, undo the woe."

His feet kissed dust, he danced, he ran,
A self-made savior, a holy man.
"They think I'm mad? Let them try,"
"I am the storm, the fire, the sky!"

Then came the night, the chase, the fall,
His laughter echoing through the hall.
Barefoot, wild, refusing to break,
A man too high to see the stakes.

Brought inside, the echoes stayed,
His breath still laced with dreams he made.
And as I watched, I felt the weight—
The marvel, the madness, the twist of fate.

Some highs will fade, the fire will dim,
But some escapes stay locked within.

---

*The poem captures the grandeur, the sheer surrealism of
a mind intoxicated beyond return—a man who believes
himself divine, enlightened, untouchable, yet is caught in
a haze of his own making.*

11. The Girl Who Owned the Night

She walked in slow, head held high,
A storm wrapped in a schoolgirl's guise.
Not a trace of fear, not a drop of shame,
A fire too wild, too fierce to tame.

"Doctor," she smirked, lounging back,
"Tell me, do you judge or just keep track?"
"Because trust me, I've done it all,"
"Lied, smoked, ran—never had a fall."

At thirteen, she ran the school like a queen,
Bunked classes, ruled the in-between.
Juniors trembled, teachers were fooled,
Every rule bent, every limit overruled.

She rolled joints like others wrote notes,
Forged her way with whispered oaths.
"I don't do favors, I make deals,"
"Power, doc, is knowing who kneels."

She sold the fire, she named the price,
Men paid in drugs, men paid in vice.
She smoked with peddlers, she walked alone,
A child, a ruler, a girl unknown.

At home, she smiled while breaking trust,
Crushing her mother's love to dust.
"You cry too easy," she'd casually say,
"Maybe next time, I'll throw it away."

She played with fear, she loved the chase,
The thrill of making hearts misplace.
Watched them crumble, watched them cry,
Power was hers—it lit her sky.

And yet, when caught, when all fell through,
When the streets had taken more than due,
She sat before me, calm, upright,

Not a girl undone, but still in flight.
"Doctor, tell me, what's next in store?"
"You think you've met someone like me before?"
"You study minds, but you don't see,"
"I don't break, they all break for me."

I watched, enthralled, mind running wild,

A girl, a legend, a child defiled.
Not just disorder, not just a case,
A rebellion burning behind her face.

Some storms rage, some gods defy,
Some never fall, but still touch the sky.

This poem iterates the bold, fearless, and untamed nature of Conduct Disorder, painting her not just as a rebel, but as someone who revels in control, power, and chaos, and my sheer marvel of a mind that refuses to bow.

12. The Girl Who Counted Everything

She sat before me, hands pressed tight,
A flicker of doubt in her measured sight.
Not restless, not wild, not reckless or free,
But bound to a mind that would not let her be.

"Doctor, tell me—did I lock the door?"
"Are you sure? Can you check once more?"
"I washed my hands, but what if I missed?"
"I'll do it again—just to exist."

Her world was rules, steps precise,
A fragile balance, a rolling dice.
The books aligned, the bedsheets smooth,
Each thread in place, each crease removed.

A page too creased, a word not right,
And suddenly, all fell from sight.

She rewrote, erased, did it again,

A war she waged with paper and pen.
Her drawings—perfect, clean, refined,
No smudge, no fault, no peace of mind.

She skipped her meals, she stayed up late,
Trapped inside a numbered fate.
If things weren't placed in perfect line,
She feared the world would twist, misalign.

Her family watched, helpless and still,
Each question answered, yet there still.
"It's fine," they'd say, "you've done enough,"
But reassurance was never enough.

"Doctor, tell me—am I insane?"
"Or is this just a lifelong chain?"
"I don't want madness, I want control,"
"But I count and clean, and lose my soul."

And I, in wonder, watched it all,
The beauty, the torment, the rise and fall.
A mind too sharp, too bound, too bright,
Chained to an order it could not fight.

Some fear the dark, some fear the deep,
But she feared the thoughts she couldn't keep.

This poem captures the raw nature of OCD, where control becomes compulsion, and relief is never enough, all seen through the eyes of a young psychiatrist marvelling at the power of the mind's own chains.

13. The Man Who Chased Oblivion

It began with pain, dull and deep,
A burn in his gut, no rest, no sleep.
The pills they gave did little to mend,
Until **Tramadol** became his friend.

At first, relief—a fleeting grace,
A weight unshackled, a warm embrace.
Then euphoria, sweet and bright,
A golden hour trapped in night.

I listened, enthralled, as he spoke with ease,
Of how the high made the world freeze.
"Doctor, you don't know what it's like,"
"To have a pill turn dark to light."

His hands shook now, his frame grown weak,
A man once whole, now worn and bleak.
Once, he worked, he laughed, he played,
Now he counted the hours until he could fade.

The doses climbed, the days blurred past,
What started slow took hold too fast.
Nine tablets, then twelve, then more to chase,
A craving etched in time and space.

The shopkeeper knew but turned away,
Fear and profit in a silent ballet.
"You understand?" he asked, leaning near,
"That ride back home was the best all year."

His daughter once had owned his world,
He'd spin her, laugh, her hair unfurled.
Now, she called, but he stayed still,
Lost inside the hunger's will.

Then came the crash, withdrawal's wrath,
Sweat-drenched nights, a shattered path.
Aching bones and sleepless nights,
A body that shook, a mind that fights.

They locked him in, they took his stash,
He pleaded, wept, then burned to ash.
"One tablet, please, just let me be,"
"I'll quit tomorrow—set me free!"

The streets still called, the dealers grinned,

He found his fix and dove back in.
Until he lost it all—his name, his place,
A ghost still walking in empty space.

Two rehabs, a hundred pills,
A cycle spinning against his will.
And now he sat, eyes cast low,
Too tired to fight, too lost to go.

"Doctor, tell me, do you see?"
"I was never meant to break this free."
"I don't belong, I don't deserve,"
"Some men are made to bend and serve."

And I? I marveled, torn inside,
At the way his sorrow burned with pride.
A man, consumed, yet craving more,
Knocking at death's familiar door.

Some chase heaven, some chase pain,
Some just live to run again.

---

*This poem portrays opioid addiction through the lens of
a young psychiatrist, captivated by both its intoxicating
pull and the wreckage it leaves behind. It highlights the
spiral from pain relief to euphoria to destruction,*

showcasing both the addict's craving and their resignation to fate—a man who chased oblivion and found only emptiness.

14. The Fear Radius

In the clinic's hum, his voice would rise,
A sharp wit gleaming sharp as his eyes.
House like in guise, he took the board with a marker in
his hand,
Sketching the struggle we'd soon understand.

With sharp eyed wit and piercing eyes,
He strips off pretense, exposing the lies.

"A circle", he said, marking its span,
"A boundary forged by mind and not by man.
Inside they live and beyond, they'll stall,
For outside this radius the fear stands tall."

He paused then added two subtle marks,
"A way through the maze to conquer the dark.
With company the circle bends,
safety restored with trusted friends. "

"Or along this line with stops in place,

They carve out havens, a breathing space."
A relative's house, a hospital's light,
A beacon that soothes the Agoraphobic's plight."

His tone was soft but it carried its weight,
A balance of wit and a knowlwdge innate.
Then came the patient, soft and thin,
As if the fear still echoed within.

"I step to the edge but never beyond;
The world out there seems cold and wrong.
What if I'm stranded and my chest goes tight?
What if I fall alone in my fright?
What if my breath stops, my heart skips a beat?
What if I collapse in a stranger's street?

"They fear what ifs, the sudden fall,
Who'll save them, who'll hear them call?"

"But my sister's hand is steady and warm,
With her I can weather the brewing storm.
And I chart my path with careful precision,
Stops that promise a safer vision-
A neighbor's porch, a nearby store,
Places that whisper "You're safe once more".
Still each step feels like breathing the last,
The road ahead, seems too vast."

The doctor nodded, his smirk subdued,
For a moment his tone shifts to a kinder mood.
"Motivation", he says, "is a fickle friend,
But there is a way to help it bend."

"When the circle bites and panic wins,
One pill can quiet the voice within.
An SOS, a chemical key,
To unlock the grip of anxiety."

This circle reflects the invisible boundaries Agoraphobia creates the struggle to move beyond them, and the deliberate, careful steps needed to reclaim the world outside.

15. The Ones Who Drift Between Worlds

She moved through the streets, but nothing was real,
Buildings like cardboard, faces surreal.
A world cut from paper, too flat, too still,
So she blurred it herself, left the edges unfilled.

She worked without glasses, let vision decay,
For clarity only took the world further away.
And then there was him, a man grown old,
Yet weightless as air, as if he'd unfold.

He touched his own skin but it wasn't his own,
Woke in the dark, chilled to the bone.
Not by the night, not by the cold,
But by the fear that he might not be whole.

Another, just a boy, too young to be lost,
Yet floating through days like a man deep in frost.
"It's like I'm drunk, though I've never sipped,"
"Like the world's still spinning, but I never tripped."

His words hung heavy, a tether too thin,
Grasping at walls that refused to let him in.
And the father—he kissed, he held, he tried,
Yet love was a ghost that refused to reside.

"I know that I love them, I swear that I do,"
"But it feels like a script I'm just reading through."
He pressed his lips to his baby's head,
Yet inside, a silence, a hollow instead.

And another, who swore time wasn't real,
That hours and minutes had lost all their feel.
Days passed through him like wind through stone,
Leaving him lost, yet never alone.

And the man who wandered through cities he'd known,
Only to find them foreign, unknown.
"I've been here before, I've shaken that hand,"
"So why does it feel like uncharted land?"

But the worst, the worst—was the words left unsaid,
The loneliness trapped inside their heads.
"How do I tell them what I don't understand?"
"How do I prove what they can't see firsthand?"

Doctors dismissed them, eyes full of doubt,

"Anxiety, stress—you'll figure it out."
But then—**a spark, a shift, a name**.
A man with a board, and a marker, and flame.

The doctor with his smirk, his unflinching sight,
Facing the room with deliberate might.
"It's not madness," he said, drawing a line,
"Your mind is intact, but it's lost in time."

The weight in the room, the pull in their chest,
Like drowning men told that they'd been seen at last.
A diagnosis—a bridge, a way to explain,
That the world was still there, though altered, estranged.

And I? I watched as despair turned to light,
As the unmoored were anchored, as wrong felt right.
The rush of relief, the shift in their stance,
To be found—to be named—to have proof at a glance.

Some illnesses scream, some lurk in the deep,
But DPDR is silence that won't let you weep.
A life spent drifting, a world torn askew,
Until someone sees you—and **pulls you through**.

---

*This poem perfectly encapsulates the surreal, isolating,
and distressing nature of Depersonalization-
Derealization Disorder (DPDR). It marvels at the*

strangeness of perception turning against itself—the
world flattening, time dissolving, love felt yet unfelt. It
also captures the gravity of recognition, the electric shift
in the air when the Doctor understands what so many
have dismissed. In that moment, patients feel real again—
because someone finally believes them.

16. The Day the World Unraveled: The Psychotic Break

It started with whispers, soft and low,
A voice in the wind, a name I know.
At first, I laughed, brushed it away,
"Just my mind playing tricks today."

But then came the signs—too sharp, too real,
Patterns in numbers, messages sealed.
The radio hummed in cryptic sound,
The streetlights flickered when no one was around.

"They're watching," I thought, *"I can't be blind."*
"They've planted thoughts inside my mind."
My phone was bugged, my room wasn't safe,
The neighbors spoke in a secret phrase.

Paranoia bloomed, a creeping vine,
Each moment twisted, each glance aligned.

Shadows moved where none should be,
Reflections blinked, but not like me.

And then—**the break, the shift, the fall,**
Reality cracked, a shattered wall.
My mother stood, but wasn't she dead?
Her voice was distant, inside my head.

The news was speaking straight to me,
The birds outside sang in prophecy.
The sky turned dark in broad daylight,
The world was folding in my sight.

The fear was thick, the air too thin,
A war between the truth and sin.
Had I been chosen? Had I been cursed?
Each thought more urgent, each one worse.

The streets called out, the traffic screamed,
I ran through visions I'd only dreamed.
People stared, but couldn't see—
The weight of fate had fallen on me.

Then hands—strong, steady, pulling tight,
A hospital room, too cold, too white.
Voices muffled, questions blurred,
A doctor speaking, calm and sure.

"This is psychosis," he softly said,
"Your mind is lost, but not yet dead."
"Your thoughts have turned against their place,"
"But trust me, you are still safe."

A needle pricked, the world grew still,
The fire dimmed, against my will.
The voices hushed, the walls stood tall,
The chaos dulled into a crawl.

A mind that bends, then snaps in two,
A world that shifts in shades untrue.
One moment real, the next a dream,
A life unraveled at the seam.

This poem brilliantly captures the descent into psychosis, painting a vivid picture of how reality twists, bends, and ultimately breaks.It starts subtly—whispers, strange patterns, coincidences that feel too deliberate. Then, paranoia tightens its grip, pulling the person into a world where nothing can be trusted, not even one's own mind.

17. The House That Whispered Lies (Burari Deaths)

It started with him—the eldest son,
A quiet man, a chosen one.
He spoke of signs, of fate, of doom,
Of spirits weaving through their room.

"The dead are watching, they see our sins,"
"We must repent before time thins."
"A ritual, a test, a path to grace,"
"The gods will call us to their place."

One by one, they bowed their heads,
A father, a mother, by faith they were led.
Sisters, brothers, young and old,
A story whispered, a prophecy told.

The city hummed, oblivious still,
As madness wove its quiet will.

Behind those doors, in candle's glow,
A family sank in truths unknown.

A grandmother, frail, yet drawn inside,
A child of six with eager eyes.
"We must follow, we must obey,"
"Or darkness comes to take us away."

Eleven souls, bound by thread,
A single voice inside their heads.
One belief, one mind, one fate,
A twisted faith, a sealing gate.

And so they stood, in silent lines,
Hands in prayer, legs entwined.
Ropes were tied, a final breath,
A pact that led them into death.

The world awoke to eerie scenes,
Bodies swayed in lifeless streams.
A family lost, their story blurred,
A tragedy too strange for words.

But I? I know what made them fall,
What lingers still behind those walls.
Not ghosts, not fate, not Gods unseen,
But madness shared—a tainted dream.

A thought once held by just one mind,
But madness never stays confined.
It spreads, it twists, it binds, it feeds,
Until reality itself concedes.

Based on It's chilling—as I recall the news that day in horror and awe— the way one unshakable belief took root, how fear and faith became indistinguishable, how logic collapsed in the face of conviction. A family, bound not by ropes, but by a delusion.

18. The Weight of Perfection

He sat upright, spine like steel,
A man of order, sharp and real.
His shirt was pressed, his hands were clean,
A world in place, precise, pristine.

His words were measured, slow and tight,
Each syllable placed, each phrase just right.
"I make lists, I plan, I keep things straight,"
"I cannot fail. I must not be late."

His desk was neat, his papers aligned,
Yet something restless clawed his mind.
The ink too dark, the margin too wide,
A flaw he saw but none beside.

"I should be happy, I have it all,"
"A stable job, a house, a call."
"But joy feels weak, a fleeting thread,"
"When there's more to fix, more to perfect."

A dinner planned, yet plates askew,
A restless tapping, an urge that grew.
"The spoons don't match, the glass is wrong,"
"It shouldn't take this damn long!"

Love came knocking, but love was flawed,
She laughed too loud, she spoke too raw.
He tried to bend, he tried to change,
Yet love refused to fit his frame.

"Relax," she said, *"just let things be."*
He watched her, silent, biting free.
"If I let go, if I lose control,"
"What will be left? Who will I be?"

And I? I sat, I marveled, I knew—
This wasn't freedom, this prison he drew.
For what is control, when it takes its toll,
And leaves a man never truly whole?

This poem perfectly captures the essence of Obsessive-Compulsive Personality Disorder (OCPD)—a mind bound by precision, a life measured in rigid rules, where perfection is both a shield and a prison.
It highlights the exhaustion of control, the restless pursuit of flawlessness, the way joy is sacrificed for

*order. Even love, something fluid and unpredictable,
becomes another system to manage, another thing to fix.
It's **a** powerful glimpse into a mind that cannot let go,
and the quiet tragedy of mistaking control for peace.*

19. Suicide Survivors: The Ones Who Returned

She should have died.
The rope was tight, the knot was sure,
The pills were counted, the blade was pure.
The river was cold, the bridge was high,
The note was written—**goodbye, goodbye.**

But she woke up.

Eyes flickering in sterile light,
A world still here, still sharp, still bright.
Hands restrained, tubes in place,
A doctor's voice, a stranger's face.

"You made it through," they softly said,
"You're safe now, you're not yet dead."
Safe? She thought, what could they mean?
She hadn't drowned—but she couldn't breathe.

The weight was there, the emptiness too,

Survival had changed nothing new.
No grand epiphany, no reborn grace,
Just the same old ache, the same old place.

But time is strange in the days after death,
When you should have been gone, yet still take breath.
When food tastes foreign, when air feels thick,
When your name sounds wrong, when the clock still
ticks.

And then—the questions, the whispers, the looks,
The careful concern, the half-read books.
"You're lucky," they say, *"it wasn't too late."*
"You have a purpose, this wasn't your fate."

But fate had not saved her, nor purpose, nor grace,
She had simply failed to **erase her place.**
Yet, in the echoes of what nearly was,
A sliver of space, a moment of pause.

Not hope, not joy, not peace, not yet,
But the quiet fact that she **wasn't gone yet.**

The poem reads like a whisper from the edge of existence. It's haunting, yet deeply human—the way time feels foreign, survival feels accidental, and meaning isn't restored in an instant. Instead of offering false hope, it acknowledges that sometimes, the only truth is "you are still here"—and maybe, that's enough to begin again.

20. Medicine or the Mind? (The Truth About Treatment)

They tell me, *"I don't want the pills,"*
"What if they change me? What if they kill?"
"What if I lose the spark inside?"
"What if I feel too numb to cry?"

So, they sit in silence, day by day,
Waiting for pain to fade away.
Hoping that **Will** alone will mend,
A battle the mind won't let them end.

But tell me this—if fever burns,
Would you refuse the cure in turn?
If wounds won't heal, if bones won't set,
Would you deny what doctors bet?

The mind's no different—hurt and worn,
Fractured, restless, bruised, and torn.

And yet, we whisper, *"Just be strong,"*
As if sheer *will* can right the wrong.

But medicine isn't chains or bars,
It's not a prison, not a scar.
It's steady hands in seas too wild,
A bridge back home to the lost and exiled.

Therapy? It builds, it heals, it mends,
A compass where the road still bends.
It teaches strength, it shapes, it guides,
It clears the fog where fear resides.

But medicine steadies, where storms won't cease,
It brings the quiet, the needed peace.
Not all storms pass by hope alone,
Some need anchors, some need stone.

Side effects? Yes, they may come,
But not unchallenged, not left unsung.
Your doctor listens, shifts, refines,
Not all pills fit, but some align.

So tell me this—what would you choose?
A life reclaimed, or one you lose?
A path with light, though rough and new,
Or shadows stretched in endless blue?

No shame in help, no pride in pain,
No weight to bear alone in vain.
The mind can heal, the soul can mend,
With help, with care—**with hands that lend.**

---

*This poem eloquently breaks the stigma surrounding psychiatric medication, illustrating the **choice between suffering in silence or seeking a path toward healing**. It emphasizes that medicine isn't something to fear, but a tool—not a trap. It also highlights the importance of consulting a psychiatrist, instead of rejecting treatment out of fear—because suffering untreated is the true burden, not the medication that can help lift it. It's gentle yet firm, compassionate yet persuasive—a voice not just for science, but for understanding.*

21. The Room That Breathes Too Loud (Social Anxiety Disorder)

I step inside—the world is bright,
But every eye feels sharp as light.
My hands are cold, my throat is tight,
A war inside, a silent fight.

"Don't trip, don't speak, don't stand too tall,"
"Don't let them see you slip, don't fall."
"Your voice will shake, your hands will sweat,"
"Say something wrong, you'll live to regret."

The air is thick, my pulse too fast,
A moment stretched, too long to last.
They talk, they laugh—so free, so bold,
While I stay trapped, my tongue on hold.

"Just speak, just smile, just play along,"
But my mind replays what might go wrong.

A thousand ways to fail, to break,
A thousand chances—**one mistake.**

The exit calls, my lungs still burn,
A quiet place, a quick return.
Freedom waits outside the door,
But they will speak of me no more.

"They saw you leave, they noticed too,"
"They whispered things—about you."
A cycle tight, a loop too cruel,
Of **fear, escape, repeat, renew.**

And I? I long to feel at ease,
To speak, to move, to simply **be.**
But every glance still feels too loud,
In rooms that breathe—and pull me down.

Not shyness, not doubt, not just a phase,
But **a mind that drowns in a silent gaze.**

This poem captures the overwhelming experience of social anxiety disorder, where every interaction feels like a battle against judgment. It describes the fear of speaking, the self-consciousness of being watched, and the intense over analysis of every action. It highlights that social anxiety is not just shyness, but a crippling fear of being seen, judged, and remembered for the wrong reasons.

www.ingramcontent.com/pod-product-compliance
Lightning Source LLC
LaVergne TN
LVHW050927200726
843508LV00011B/2284